LUCIANO BERTI

ALL THE WORKS OF

MICHELANGELO

AND SISTINE CHAPEL

Translated by
SUSAN GLASSPOOL

BONECHI EDITORE FIRENZE

REFERENZE FOTOGRAFICHE:

Foto Alinari: 3-14-28-29-49-50-52-53-54-64-65-66-67-69

Foto Barone: 5-12-13-30-38-39-40-41-42-43-44-45-46-47-48
55-61-62

Foto Bruno del Priore: 17-18-19-20-21-22-23-24-25-26-27
57-58

Foto Marzari: 1-2-4-10-11-15-33-34-35-36 51-63

Foto Scala: 6-16-37-56-58-59-60-70

Direttore Responsabile VITTORIO CUMINETTI
Condirettore   GIAMPAOLO BONECHI

Type setting by - GENERAL PRINTING COMPANY LTD. - Yokohama – Japan
Stampa - ARTI GRAFICHE PARIGI E MAGGIORELLI - Firenze
Fotolito - LA FOTOLITOGRAFIA - Firenze

Autorizzazione del Tribunale di Firenze n. 1835 del 31-5-67
Spedizione a tariffa editoriale ridotta

INDEX OF THE WORKS

MICHELANGELO BUONARROTI

The baby that was born on March 6th 1475 in the house of the Mayor of Caprese, a small inhabited place among the rough mountains of the high Tiber valley, was destined to live long, until 1564, and — an otherwise revealing thing — to become considered as the greatest artist in all the three arts by his contemporaries, superior to all others, even those of Antiquity. To attain such a degree, and this in the golden century of the Renaissance, was certainly an extraordinary event, perhaps possible to be effected only by the fundemental choice that Michelangelo would have made in his method of concentration. He was an introvert, without a mondane quality, though notwithstanding this, he knew how to make the world bow before him.

Vasari and Condivi describe a terribly solitary man to us, with an extremely, incredibly moderate life, from his continuous and secret work from the very measured and ambiguous word, when it was not cutting, and who was able to get through to one a modest and loving person. Those who did not like his work, spoke instead of him as a misanthrope, a mean and superior enigmatic person. The Pope, the very proud Julius II, said in 1512 to Sebastiano del Piombo, « Michelangelo is terrible, as you see, that one cannot be familiar with him ».

As for sobriety, his house was almost bare, and sometimes he ate only bread, while continuing his work. A list of three menus of 1517 has been preserved, one is for himself only, and two are for when there were guests. 1) Two pieces of bread; a decanter of wine; a herring; tortellini (pasta); 2) A salad; four pieces of bread; a decanter of « tondo » and a quarter of sharp wine; a small plate of spinach; four anchovies; tortellini. 3) Six pieces of bread; two fennel soups; a herring; a decanter of « tondo ».

However, closing himself up in his visions, bearing his tiring and very hard work, and wrapping himself up in mystery, Michelangelo did not disperse the least part of his energies, revealed almost none of his most communal humanity and presented only his formidable achievements. His ambition must have been immense, but he scorned aims as banally mondane. Neither was he taken care of by the most feared and flattering 'journalistic' pen of the century, Aretino. Not even the possibility of fabulous earnings deviated him. He also feared relations with powerful people, and in 1549, already at the height of his glory, he wrote to his nephew Leonardo in search of recommendations: « I have very few affairs in Rome and do not know those who can be of help, and if I ask one of these people one thing, each of them will ask me for a thousand. However I need to be familiar with a few: I will do what I can also ».

However Michelangelo well knew how to cultivate his myth. Although modest, he had such outbursts of pride so as to make him respected even by higher authorities, used to the obsequeous servility of others. Isolated and closed he appeared to be the Artist and nothing else; Aretino wrote of him: « ... you, to be divine, do not think the society of men worthy ... ». Also the famous unfinished sense in his sculpture was perhaps a way of never saying his last word, to make one catch a glimpse of unutterable beauty, to the infinate. He made a bonfire of his drawings, « in order that » wrote Vasari — « nobody could see the labour that he endured and his ways of attempting his understanding, so as not to appear imperfect .... ». Likewise, his personality seemed to be concentrated all in an enormous expressive force, like the tormented one of his unfinished statues; and his conversation with society was limited to the dictated imperiousness of his masterpieces, burning up normal relations.

The son of a man (Ludovico), who was little capable, at the most he was the most modest state functionary like when he was sent to be Mayor of Caprese, Michelangelo also became ambitious to raise the fortunes of the Buonarroti Simoni family once more, which was of Florentine stock in ancient times and had notable rank in Florence in the past. In this he had a normal family attachment. « We are citizens descended from very noble extraction », he loved to repeat, and from 1506 he endeavoured to buy ground, deposit savings, and to arrange his nephews' marriages with aristocratic families. His nephew Leonardo would have had a conspicuous inheritance, and the Buonarroti house in the ancestral quarter of S. Croce is the material testimony of the artist's obligation in benefit of his family. His mother, Francesca, died instead when Michelangelo was only six years old, and that could have contributed to his melancholic character, or to his manner of imagining the Madonna as lacking that feminine sweetness which he had been unable to experience. Michelangelo was directed to literary studies, but soon, notwithstanding his family's opposition, who held that the artisic career was plebean, his inclination led him to the latter.

6

THE FIRST WORKS: *The Madonna of the Stair.*
The Battle of the Centaurs - The Wooden Crucifix.

Perhaps on the advice of the young painter Francesco Granacci, at the age of thirteen, in 1488, he was placed for three years in the famous Ghirlandaio's school, but he left that shop after a year (where Ghirlandaio did not favour him above the others) so as to frequent the garden of Lorenzo the Magnificent in San Marco with its splendid collection of antique statues for which the old sculptor Bertoldo was curator. The Magnificent actually welcomed him into the Medici Palace among his familiars and in the research of the intellectuals who formed the court around the lord of Florence. According to biographers, he then carried out two sculptures, which remain to this day: the ´Madonna of the Stair´ and the ´Battle of the Centaurs´.

In the Madonna (fig. no. 1), the « flat » technique is taken from Donatello, but as a whole the veiled figure is inspired by classical tombs. She dominates, however, sitting down with great bodily structure and with the classically amplified forms of the drapery all over the little bass relief, and her face is absorbed, almost dazzled, in foreboding thought. The putti in the background (three of which are on a staircase) are already holding — if one looks closely — the funeral sheet of the future Christ. The composition is tight, as in plastic nuclei, and the Madonna is always more related to the background; in the lap of the Madonna is the back of the robust baby suckling the milk, already belonging to the athletic type of Michelangeloesque figures. Also, in the studio in his first drawings, Michelangelo, above all the others, had demonstrated his instinct towards powerful and cast figures, copying them from the greatest preceding masters of Florentine painting, Giotto and Masaccio.

The Battle of the Centaurs (fig. no. 2), whose theme was suggested to the boy by Poliziano, presents other clear foretellings of the Michelangeloesque future on its face: he does not indulge in a particoloured description of the scene at all, but unitarily feels the enveloping swirling of the bodies, a view of various dynamic attitudes possible for the nude body; while the particular technique of his unfinished work, (one can see it in the barely sketched heads of hair), already seems to have been applied here, (and also in the Madonna). The youth, protected by the Magnificent, already exemplified then an art very different from the exquisite, but more chiselled fifteenth century elegance, in these two marbles, a more ponderous, more radical and more abstractly ideal vision.

When Lorenzo the Magnificent died in 1492, Michelangelo returned to his paternal home. Then he fellowed the preachings of Savonarola, which impressed him with their violent recall to a conscience of shame and the necessity of the reform of the Church. The religious sentiment, the sensibility to the disagreement between this and the pagan classical culture, and the problem of an internal rennovation of Christianity, became always stronger ideas in Buonarroti in the course of his life. However, for now, as an artist — as in the wooden

Crucifix for S. Spirito which is of recent discovery (fig. no. 4) — he indulged in experimenting in a delicate modellation of the human form, sensible in reality more to anatomical studies, (for which the prior of S. Spirito furnished him with a room and the bodies necessary for dissection), than to the dramatic spiritual revolution invoked by Fra Girolamo. The Crucifix of S. Spirito is a little effeminate in its body. There was also the statue of a Hercules from this period (1492-4), which then ended up in France and was lost.

THE FIRST STAY AWAY FROM FLORENCE: *The Angel Candelabra The Bacchus - The Pietà of Rome.*

Michelangelo was impressionable, and when he understood the situation in Florence (October 1494) of the second expulsion of the hated Piero dei Medici and political disorders, with precaution he abandoned the House of his benefactors, actually fleeing from the city. We can find written: « It is known that Michelangelo the sculptor from the Garden went to Venice without saying anything to Piero .... it seems to me that Piero took it badly ». From Venice he soon transferred to Bologna, here he spent a year as the guest of the gentleman G. F. Aldovrandi, to whom he read the great Tuscan poets (Dante, Petrarch, Boccaccio), and at this man's interest he sculpted a serene youthful Angel (fig. 3) for the Arch of S. Domenico, and also the statuettes of the Saints Petronius and Proculus, sensible to the vigorous style of Jacopo della Quercia.

At the end of '95 he returned to Florence, where the situation had become more tranquil, but he only stayed six months there, then going on to Rome where he remained until 1501. He did not work for the papal court of Alexander VI Borgia here, but was in contact with the Cardinal Riario, the banker Jacopo Galli (with whom perhaps he lived) and with the French Cardinal of S. Dionigi. The esteem which the young Buonarroti had won must have already been very great anyway if Galli was able to make such a guarantee for the Pietà: « And I, Jacopo Gallo, promise the very reverend Monsignore that the said Michelangelo will make the said work in a year, and it will be the most beautiful work of marble that there is today in Rome, and nobody can make it better than that master today ». In effect, whether it is the Bacchus or the Pietà, they are both two masterpieces. In evidence anyway, and with a complete formal perfection, Michelangelo signed the Pietà, which he did not do on any other work, a sign of his complete satisfaction.

Of the two works, one deals with a profane theme, the other sacred, according to a duality of inspiration which was already started with the Battle of the Centaurs and the Madonna of the Stair. In the Bacchus (fig. 5) there is a physical, pagan, turgid and almost ambiguous beauty, (Vasari speaks of him as « having given it the lightness of male youth and the fleshyness and roundness of a girl »). Also the result

A copy from Giotto.

of an authentically lived sensuality is also very efficatious, in the swaying pose and the hebrew face of the young god; while the calculus for a varied vision is stupendous, although always very accurate from all points of view around the statue, in a richness of curvilineal rythms which however concur also in the little satyr who steals the grapes from the god, from behind his back. One must notice also the certain symbolic significance of downfall and resumption: the god wears a tiger skin, the animal dedicated to Bacchus and which, greedy for grapes and wine, dies; but the happy satyr takes over the cycle of the joy of the senses and life.

In the Pietà (fig. 7-8-9), instead, a very young Madonna, absorbed composedly in her pain, alluding with a gesture of resignation to the divine wish with her left hand, sits in a splendid cascade of folds of her lap, and on her knees is a very beautiful body of the dead Christ, from His reclining head. The Virgin is a figure already sensible to the Leonardesque sweetness, and the pyramidal back is already typical of the sixteenth century classicism; but the lovely calligraphy in every detail is still related perhaps to the Florentine fifteenth century. In any case, one can observe that Buonarroti did not yet dare to sacrifice the beauty of the expressive violence and tragicalness, and the criticisms of his contemporaries of the excessive youthfulness of the Virgin — so much exactly, against reality, because all of it was 'beautiful' in the group — centering even this weak point ingeniously. Who would have predicted that Michelangelo would arrive at the Rondanini Pietà (fig. 70)?

THE YOUTHFUL MASTERPIECES IN FLORENCE: *The Madonna of Bruges The Pitti Tondo - The Taddei Tondo - The Doni Tondo - The David.*

From 1501 to 1505 the artist returned to Florence. Leonardo was present there then, returned from Milan, and stimulated also by that comparison with the great da Vinci, Buonarroti passed on to a more monumental and synthetic phase. Putting to one side the statuettes for the Piccolomini altar in Siena, (a commission procured again by Galli), finished by others and not very good, the series of works in this period counts a statue of the Madonna and Child (Bruges), two tondoes in sculpture on the same theme (Bargello and the Royal Academy of London), and one painted (Uffizi), a David in bronze, lost, and the gigantic one in marble today at the Academy, which should have been the first of a series of Apostles for the facade of the Duomo; and the cartoon, also lost, for a fresco in Palazzo Vecchio of the 'Battle of Cascina', in concurrence with the Battle of Anghiari by Leonardo. The artist, at a little more than twenty five years old, was able to set himself against da Vinci at fifty years old; Stendhal has imagined the comparison in this way « the ardent genius of the sculptor faced the difficulty with a kind of fury which gave pleasure to his admirers; these preferred Michelangelo who worked fast, to Leonardo who always kept promising .... ».

Study for a Madonna with St. Anne.

The Madonna of Bruges (fig. 6), with the Child standing held by
the seated but rather vertical figure of the Virgin, is linked to the Pietà
in St. Peters, but with greater severe blocking. The sculpture was sold
in 1506 to the heirs Mascheroni or Mouscron, who transferred it to
Bruges, where Dürer saw it then in 1521. In the Pitti Tondo at the
Bargello (fig. 12) and in the Taddei Tondo today in London (fig. 14),
to have represented the Madonna not in a half bust (as in fifteeth century tradition), but complete in the tondo, he fitted their concentration
into seated and angular pose, and the curvilinear rythms of the Infants
so as to agree with the bend of the slab of marble, and also the motifs
of grace which unite a certain feeling of tension in it. The Madonnas
are not of the supreme sweetness of Leonardo, nor of the harmonious
serenity which Raphael painted in Florence between 1504 and 1508,
but they are more proud and unquiet images, where the form appears
to embossed and vibrant. The marble is worked with great care and
security, rough and sketched in some parts, and in others more refined,
resulting in varied pictorial effects.

In the tondo painted for the Doni (fig. 13), the composition of
the group of the Holy Family is then made complex, and its proceeding in a spiral direction intensifies the plastic sense, inviting the eye
to turn around the volumes. In the background, nude ephebes in a
semicircle seem to allude to antique paganity, and they create an interest to the group in the foreground. Michelangelo sets himself against
Leonardesque mistyness and the fused sweetness of Raphael, in the
terse atmosphere of his painting and the dry vigour of the figures, with
clear and cold colours iridescent under the light, full and plastic forms,
that is a vision so different in all the sense of virile energy. Miracul-
ously carved, without adding any piece, from a block of marble already
injured and left abandoned forty years before at the Opera of the Duomo
and which nobody felt able to continue, he then made — fron 1501 to
1504 — the very famous David (figs. 10-11) of this pride, congenital
of the same city of Florence. In fact the David symbolises the two
civil virtues of « strength » (in the harmonic but powerful body and
the folded arm, armed by the sling), and « scorn » (in the vigil and
decided face). Only in the over subtle view of the flank can we under-
stand the difficulty that Michelangelo had to overcome, constrained
by the subtle thickness of the block to develop a prevalently frontal
vision. Finally, in the cartoon for the ' Battle of Cascina ', of the theme
Buonarroti had made a representation of Florentine soldiers surprised
by the alarm during a bathe in the Arno, a composition which was
completely formed of nudes springing up in the most divers attitudes,
fixing his concentration uniquely on the theme of human figures, against
the universal sense of Leonardo. With his new, ponderous and great
anatomism in the heroic sense, the cartoon enormously impressed the
artists of the new generations, and was fundemental towards the development of sixteenth century painting: Vasari says « that the stupid
and dead artists stayed, seeing the extremity of art in such a cartoon
as Michelangelo showed them ». In effect the cartoon was destroyed,
because afterwards various artists took possession of pieces of it as
relics.

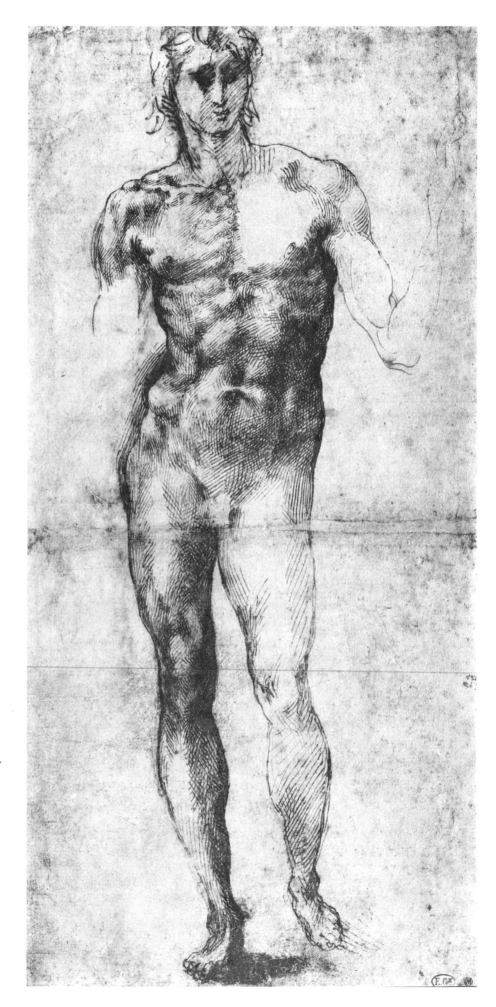

Study for a virile figure.

Study for the Battle of Cascina.

THE MEETING WITH POPE JULIUS II: *The St. Matthew*
The Sistine Chapel.

In the meantime probably Giuliano da Sangallo, the Vatican architect, informed Julius II about Michelangelo: called to Rome (1505), the Pope intrusted him with the project of his grandiose sepulcre, the tomb that the artist was to finish only after forty years and much reduced, and which seemed a tragedy in his life to him. But in the beginning the project — of a gigantic squared monument on three levels, with more than forty figures — seemed to prosper rapidly; and Michelangelo took himself off at once to extract the necessary marbles from Carrara, where eight months were taken up, dreaming up among other things of sculpting a colossus, visible from far off by sailors on a mountain. The marbles for the sepulcre were already arrived in Rome, when Michelangelo — considering himself offended by the Pontiff — abandoned it (17ᵗʰ August 1506) and fled to Florence, followed in vain by the papal emisseries.

In November he presented himself before the terrible Pope at Bologna, obtaining his pardon, but in the interval — frightened by the consequences and the pontificial pressures on the Florentine government to have him again in Rome — he even planned on emigrating to Turkey, where the sultan offered him the job of a great bridge at Constantinople. Meanwhile in Florence he was able to carry out the St. Matthew (fig. 15), which emerges unfinished from the rough block which imprisoned it, dramatic in its freedom and in the visionary's face. In Bologna, after the reconciliation, Julius II commissioned him to do the papal statue in bronze for the facade of St. Petronio, seated and in the act of benedicting, which the artist cast in 1507 and which the Bolognese destroyed when in revolt in 1511.

But in 1506 already, Pope Julius had thought of commissioning Buonarroti to fresco the vault of the Sistine Chapel, to begin with perhaps he was reluctant to give an undertaking which would distract the artist from the pontificial sepulcre, and put him to the test in a pictorial technique in which he had not had much experience. In the spring of 1508, however, the task was accepted and the artist was enthusiastic, proposing — and this was welcomed — a project which was much more complex than before; while he called some helpers from Florence, among whom was his old friend Granacci, (these he got rid of quickly, proceeding absolutely alone, and realising the work in twenty months, this is rather legendary, resulting in the verification of criticism). The preparation of the drawings and cartoons continued until January 1509; in October 1512 all was finished: in the sky of the Chapel (figs. 16 to 27), a powerful, burdensome system of false architecture was animated by a multitude of figures (around three hundred), until the nine scenes of Genesis which appear in the open pictures at the apex of the vault. At the apex, on on the other side also, there was the vision of a heroic type by Buonarroti: the gigantic figures of the Sybil and the Prophets (figs. 20-27), seated the base of the vault, they confirm a physical monumentality which is dilated even more in their visionary spirituality;

couples of very beautiful nude youthful figures flank the upper scenes with movement, contributing to an animation which is in very high increasing symphony; while the Biblical scenes are always made more synthetically grandiose the more that we advance — towards the end of the chapel where there is the altar — to the very first scenes in which the Creator himself is the protagonist with His unique formidable energy. Perhaps the supreme scene is that of the Creation of Adam (fig. 18), where the Eternal in transfused flight, through the contact of hands, gives life — as in electric current — to the powerful still torpid body of the first man created by him. In the periferic zone and at the bases of the pendentives and the lunettes (with the Ancestors of Christ) the painting of Buonarroti is rested, instead, in rapid figurisation and in whimsical, intimate and humorous tones. In a sketch in Casa Buonarroti, among others, we find an autocaricature of the painter intent on the very difficult frescoing — carried out always holding his head upwards — of the immense vault (more than 1000 sq. metres), accompanied by a bitter poem in outburst:

« *I have already got a throat doing this, suffering as cats do from water in Lombardy...* »

and with a pessimistic and disconsolate finale:

« *My dead painting defends anyway, Giovanni, and my honour does not feel in a good place, neither I a painter* ».

THE WORKS FOR THE TOMB OF JULIUS II, AND THE WORKS FOR THE MEDICI PONTIFFS IN FLORENCE: *The Prisoners of the Louvre - The Moses - The Prisoners of the Academy - The Victory - Project for the Facade of San Lorenzo - The New Sacristy - Kneeling Adolescent - The Model of Fiume - Resurrected Christ.*

Julius II died unexpectedly in 1513 and therefore his sepulcre — for which it seems that the enemies of Michelangelo had deterred him from doing the undertaking, saying that it was bad luck — returned to actuality: that year Buonarroti made a new contract and a new project with the executors of the will. Between 1513 and 1516 he then sculpted the two Prisoners (figs. 28-29) today in the Louvre, symbolic figures of the Arts imprisoned after the death of the Pontiff, where the memory of the Laocoön, discovered a short time before, acted in the tormented sense for the two young men, one rebelling in vain, the other become exhausted. The Moses (figs. 31-32), also for the Sepulcre, accompanied

Study for a senile head.

Study for a head.

them, grandiose and terrible like the Prophets of the Sistine. Quite a lot later (perhaps around 1532) — and still for that tomb, over which he was accused of unfulfilment, and which it seems that successive circumstances prevented him from finishing — Michelangelo sketched out the Four Prisoners today at the Academy (figs. 33-34-35-36), tragically oppressed by the ugly material in which they seem to fight to free themselves; and the Victory (fig. 51; today in Palazzo Vecchio), a group of two, where the young conqueror, standing over his subdued foe, looks meloncholy however and subtly anguished, almost concious of fatality and vanity. Now the very beautiful figure is however completely articulated, in a spiral rythm which has also been called snakelike; but anyway the tranquil haughtiness is far away and the ideal aesthetic is more elaborate and tormented.

In the meantime in Florence, (let us return to the second decennium of the sixteenth century), the Medici rule was re-established, and a Medici was also the new Pope Leo X, who had known Michelangelo for a long time, but who preferred to use him somewhere other than in Rome — where Raphael held sway anyway — actually in Florence. In 1516 the artist was given the commission of planning the facade for the Medici basilica of S. Lorenzo (the model is in the Buonarroti House, compare fig. 52), which he designed in his usual grandiosity as a powerful combination of architecture and sculpture, and for which he spent years quarrying marble in Versilia. However this project was never realised because of the lack of sufficient funds, but was substituted by that of a new funerary chapel, associated to the same S. Lorenzo; the New Sacristy (from 1520). For this he dealt above all with Cardinal Giulio dei Medici, the next Clement VII, who had the merit of having made Buonarroti realise this mass, notwithstanding every difficulty which intervened, and of having given him substantial liberty: « he says that he knows that you intend much more than him, and he will leave you to do it alone ».

The Sacristy should have been a funerary chapel of the Medici, those risen anyway to princely and papal range, to hold the corpses of Lorenzo the Magnificent and his brother Giuliano (who was assassinated in the Pazzi conspiracy); moreover that of Giuliano Duke of Nemours (died 1516) and that of Lorenzo Duke of Urbino (died 1519) — two princes who showed promise which they were never able to use from the House of the Medici — and finally, the bodies of the Pontiffs Leo X and Clement VII also. However Michelangelo transcended the aulic pompousness of the theme, and resulted in showing more solemn and universal values. Meanwhile, he resumed the scheme for the Old Sacristy by Brunelleschi, in this way binding it to a more antique and sober Florentine tradition; then, in the statuary figures, rather than celebrating the powerful, he manifested a high and impersonal meditation on human destiny and vanity, until being appeased in religious ideality, (figs. 41-42, 45-46). Condivi, in his days spoke of expressions of « Time which consumes all ». A current interpretation (Tolnay) sees a reassumed image of the Universe in the Chapel, with its three spheres placed one above the other. Of the three zones of architecture, the inferior part with the tombs would represent the Hades of the dead; the intermediary zone (2nd order) — of a more calm and rational architecture — the terrestrial sphere; and finally, the more high and luminous zone, with the large lunettes and the dome with its radiating coffering, the celestial vault. On the two sepulcres, the pairs of statues (Day and Night; Dawn and Dusk), in their turn signify in the inexorable passing of the hours with death following, and would have provoked the break in the centre of the covers of the sepulcre from which it seems « the immortal spirit of the deceased is liberated [the statues of the two princes] so as to lift themselves up into a region inaccessible to the blind forces of Time ». The spirit is found again there in its true essence « in the eternal contemplation of the idea of life, symbolised by the Virgin and the Child »: both the statues of the two princes in fact look towards this sculpture, which is placed at the side in front of the altar. On the other hand, other interpretations have been proposed, but certainly the powerful but also sorrowful figures of the Hours, and the Thinker of the two princes, signify a solemn conception of death, beyond every contingency. For example, the story is famous that Michelangelo, to those who observed to him that his statue (fig. 45) was not like Duke Giuliano, replied that anyway, after ten centuries, nobody would be aware of it. Rather, the idealising sublimation is so great that, in the statues of the New Sacristy, one can read the most contrary intentions and contents, continuing with Giuliano, for example, the volitive and violent despot or else the antimachiavellian prince and model of moral equilibrium, the *vir activus* and very handsome, or the undecided and the consumptive can be seen; in this way the same phsycological signification results as ambiguous and polyvalent. The Kneeling-Youth (fig. 50) of Leningrad (not, however, of very certain authenticity), and the Fiumes, of which there is a model in the Casa Buonarroti (fig. 49) should also have made a part of the set.

Many things changed in the rest of it during around fifteen years in which the work continued, and Michelangelo, who had started it under the protection of the Medici, but was at the same time faithful to the Italian sixteenth century civilization at its apex, was determined by the anti-Medici republic, and, after Rome had undergone the terrible and profane Sacking, and Florence was then dominated by the Imperial armies and papal relations. But meanwhile we have not yet remembered the Resurrected Christ (fig. 37), which he carried out (1519-21) in a second version for Metello Vari in Rome, a work which rather feels the effect again of antique sculpture, almost in contrast to the profane statuary forms as in the Greco-Roman styles, and the religious attributes (the cross etc.) are also expressions of Christ. On the other hand, this work once more also uses the experiences of Leonardo.

Other than the New Sacristy, he then had (from 1523) from Clement VII the commission for the construction of the Laurentian Library in Florence, still associated to the block of the Medici convent

Madonna suckling her Son.

Cleopatra.

of S. Lorenzo. Finished much later, the Library is an example, together with the Sacristy, of a new conception of architecture, with his Vestibule (fig. 53), where the staircase breaks forth in a cascade and the columns are set with a force that almost dig out the walls in general movement which seems to anticipate Baroque; while the very long Hall, with the plutei-tables for the precious codexes, is thickly and decoratively pronounced. If one also wishes to perceive a symbolic value in this counter-opposition between the Vestibule, lower and more tormented, and the Upper Hall: « the contrast between the two atmospheres, impersonates that of the battles and aspirations of the external world [the Vestibule] with the ordinated unfolding of studies, and in the upper level [the Hall] speculations and literary leasure ». (De Angelis d'Ossat).

MICHELANGELO IN THE DEFENCE AND THE DEFEAT OF HIS CITY:
The Fortifications of Florence - The David Apollo.

Omitting other minor architectural works, in this way we arrive at 1527 when Rome was sacked, and in Florence the Medici party fell and the old Republic returned. Michelangelo, whose intimate sentiments were Republican exactly, placed himself at its disposition, in view of the defence assumed the direction of the fortifications, for which he was nominated Governor at the beginning of 1529. In the summer of that year he was invited on a mission to Ferrara to study the fortifications there, and it was then that he promised Duke Alfonso the cartoon for a Leda, (lost but noted by replicas). To defend the gates of Florence, he then designed singular bastions, which even now remind one of the structure of crustaceans, with 'trunnions' and bulwarks, (fig. 54). Some judge that he allowed for the development of the heary artillary, but there are instead the witnessed criticisms of his contemporaries as to their little practical efficiency. The already current voices of treachery and defeat frightened the very sensitive Buonarroti however, who fled to Venice in the September, and was condemned by the Republic: in the meantime the city was tight with the siege from the enemy. But Michelangelo returned there and his final behaviour was couragious: and when finally, Florence capitulated, in August of 1530, he hid in the tower of S. Niccolò, and the police searched for him in vain at his home as far as the lavatory.

However Pope Clement pardoned the artist, because he went back to the sculpture in the New Sacristy: Michelangelo carried it out (1530-1534), « pushed more from fear than by love » (Condivi), bitterly throwing himself upon the marbles with a rythm which gave rise to fears for his health. « It has been said that you are working day and night » wrote (1531) his friend Sebastiano del Piombo to him; and shortly afterwards: « And he [Clement VII] was amazed, when he read your letter in my presence that the said figures are finished, he said that there had never been a major worker than you, when you want to ... And he called me again and said: write to him that I beg him to take his work more easily, and that he does only what he can, as I do not wish that any disturbance should come about... some illness... and he said that sometimes you should go for a walk... ». Michelangelo also had to carry out a sculpture for the hard pontificial commissary, Baccio Valori, of the Apollo-David (fig. 38) which is now in the Bargello, a delicate 'snakelike' figure; and for the Marquis del Vasto he had to do the cartoon of a 'Noli me tangere', and also his friend Bartolomeo Bettini that of a 'Venus and Cupid' (known from the derivations). We have records also, that in 1532 a new contract was made for the tomb of Julius II and it is from then that the four Slaves of the Academy and the Victory of the Palazzo Vecchio come.

MICHELANGELO LEAVES FLORENCE: *The Last Judgement* *The Bust of Brutus.*

But in Florence, Michelangelo, fearful of the young and violent Duke Alessandro, who was hostile to him, in 1534 (when his father died at the age of 91), he left the city definately, moving to Rome. Here, after Clement VII, Paul III Farnese (1534-49) highly valued the artist; here he would have been received in the circle of the most eminent Florentine exiles; here was the very handsome aristocrat, Tommaso Cavalieri, for whom Buonarroti conceived an authentic passion; and here he would have then met Vittoria Colonna. At the age of sixty, Michelangelo wrote letters and poems of platonic love to Cavalieri, and carried out very refined drawings with mythological themes for him, alluding to his feeling: on Ganymede, Tizio, The Fall of Phaethon, Archers, Bacchanalia of putti, and « divine head » because Cavalieri « was learning to draw ». Cavalieri was one of the motives which led him to make his home in Rome.

Meanwhile Paul III at once entrusted him with the frescoing of the two headings to the Sistine Chapel: on the walls of the entrance should have been the Fall of the Rebelling Angels (not carried out); on the other wall the 'Last Judgement' (figs. 56-57-58. The cartoons for this were ready in 1535, while the painting, carried out all by his own hand by the master alone, was uncovered on the eve of All Saints in 1541. The fresco was received with hyperbolic phraises, but reservations were not left out because of the complete nudity and other liberties. N. Sernini, for example, wrote to a cardinal: « a great and difficult work, seeming to be more that five hundred [in realty there are a little less than four hundred] figures and types that if another painter tried to do just one of figures, he would be unable. Even if the work is of that beauty which Your Worship thinks, it does not lack people who condemn it; the Very Reverend Order of the Chietini are the first who say that the nudes do not look right in such a place, that show their bareness... others say that he has done Christ without a beard and too young... ». Above all, the malicious Pietro Aretino, offended because Michelangelo had not followed some of his advice for the composition, pretended to be scandalised, writing to him: « your figures would have been better in a delicious bath (the place of pleas-

Study for a resurrected Christ

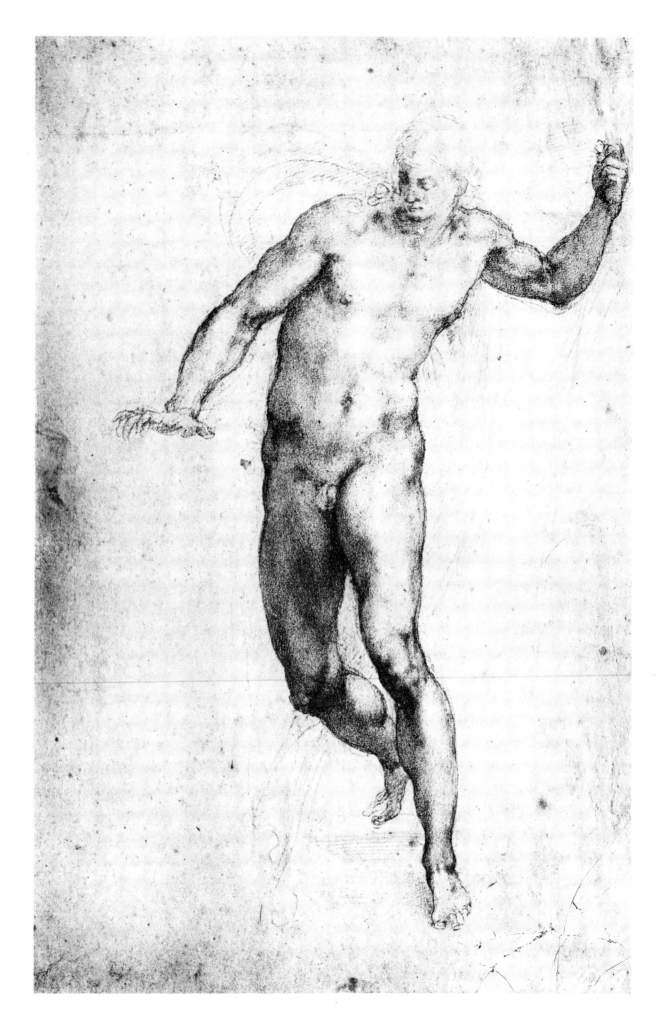

ures) than in a Supreme Court... ». In 1564 orders were given, in effect, to cover any « obscene » parts of the painting.

But in reality nothing could have been more severe and tragic than the Michelangeloesque vision. From the striking gesture of the athletic Christ, who is similar to a Young Man but beardless like an Apollo, all the Last Event takes a swirling motion, in great groupings of figures between pauses of emptyness, almost in the thickened and loosely broken feeling of thundery clouds. Low down on the left, woken by a platoon of horn blowing angels underneath Christ, the dead are returning to life from the earth, and those chosen for the divine force are attracted towards the heights; those already damned fall or are thrown desperately to the bottom, where the boat of Charon with his load of livid sinners, is ferried towards the abyss; in the right hand corner is Minos. High up in the lunette, on the contrary, whirling angels make the signs of the Passion, in remorse for human conscience; and the Apostles, Martyrs and Saints are pressed in a mass around Christ, where a frightened and pious Virgin is enclosed. On the skin of St. Bartholomew is the grotesque self portrait of the painter. The colour has left the variety of the Sistine Vault reduced to two dominating notes of the brown of the bodies on the background of the sky; the perspective is exelled (the figures high up reach 2,50 metres, and those low down 1,55 metres); the powerful anatomical forms appear subdued, however by the spiritual fate; the melodic beauty of the lineal contours runs across in a symphonic expression, powerful and overwhelming of the awfulness and the tragicalness. Really Michelangelo now, when they were trying to accuse him of heresy, profoundly felt the religious problem, the anguish of sin, and the sublimity of the Divine; in this way he intimately took part in the Judgement, and emotively lived the hour, preoccupying himself little with exterior conveniences. When, later, Daniele da Volterra was ordered by Paul IV to veil the more scabrous parts of the nudes, Buonarroti only sarcastically commented that « His Holiness minds putting the world in order, because arranging a painting is a thing of small count ».

During the frescoing of the Judgement, Michelangelo also sculpted the bust of 'Brutus', (today at the Bargello, fig. 55), on inspiration from the literary and exiled politician Donato Giannotti, for the Cardinal Ridolfi. The portrait of the tyrant is positively seen, disdainful and commanding in the face arranged in profile: the bust is inspired by the antique ones of the Roman Emperors, particularly that of Caracalla. Someone has suggested that it deals with an ideal portrait of Lorenzino dei Medici: he had killed the Duke Alessandro in 1537 in Florence, and all the people who were anti-Medici had taken his side because of this.

PAINTING AND SCULPTURE OF HIS OLD AGE: *The Conversion of St. Paul*
*The Crucifixion of St. Peter - The Pietà of Santa Maria del Fiore - The
Pietà of Palestrina - The Rondanini Pietà.*

In 1542-45 the tomb of Julius II was finally finished, but in a very
much reduced manner, according to a project which was anyway the
sixth successive one, placing it in S. Pietro in Vincoli: the Slaves did
not form a part of it anymore; neither did the Victory, and there
remained only the gigantic Moses, flanked by 'Rachel' and 'Leah',
(one cannot deny that there is a certain coldness about these works);
plus other figures by helpers. Between 1542 and 1550, inside the
Pauline Chapel, Buonarroti frescoed two great lateral spaces with the
'Conversion of St. Paul' and the 'Crucifixion of St. Peter' (figs. 59-
60): the first still close to the style of the Judgement, however, both
with an abstract excitement which has a perplexing result, notwithstanding the attempts of more recent criticisms for the revaluation of
these extreme paintings. Certainly they experience that crisis of personality of the old Michelangelo, the 'conversion' according to a religious
vision influenced by the circle of Vittoria Colonna; of a formal research
which is difficult and extreme, it looks anyway, not towards external
progress but to the internal, spiritual and expressionistic searchings. It
has been said that the frescoes wished to show two general moments
of the intimate religiosity of the believer, exactly the convert and the
martyr.

In the circle of the Colonna, who died in 1547, in fact, the religious,
reformist ideas of Valdès, Ochino etc. circulated, that is, the doctrine
of the justification of faith alone, and the pessimism instead around the
possibility of the salvation of the soul by means of one acting virtue.
Michelangelo now adhered to these propositions, which were already
in his poetry, for example:

« *To ascend without grace is a thought in vain...* ».

Feeling painfully the incapacity of the spirit to reach an authentic
religiosity without divine help:

« *I love you* [*o God*] *with my tongue and then I mourn
that Love does not reach the heart; neither do I know well
from where*

The door opens to grace... »
« *...from when the pen
does not correspond to the work and makes the page a liar* ».

(It must be noted that he did not leave out works of charity also,
as to the modest poor, or he furnished dowries for girls without means).
This sense of an almost desperate religious anxiety is also expressed
in drawings like the very beautiful late series (around 1555), for a
Crucifixion — developed from a precedent 'Crucifixion', for Vittoria

28　　*The sacrifice of Abraham.*

Study for a Crucifix between two grieving.

29

Colonna, now lost — and is expressed in the sculptoral groups of the three Pietàs.

In the Pietà of Santa Maria del Fiore (1550-55 circa; figs. 61-62) — originally carried out by the Master for his tomb in S. Maria Maggiore in Rome; and in which this time the marble is broken under the working of artists (it was adjusted by Calcagni, to whom we owe the completion of the Magdalen) — the figure of Christ is bent, as if broken, at the leg, and the arms of the body are extended in a disarticulated arch, supported by a Madonna, with her face only just sketched out, and the kneeling Magdalen. The conical group, from the painfully angular lines, and the rude plastic masses, culminated in the figure of Joseph of Arimathea, hooded, a self portrait of Michelangelo himself. The artist is figured next to Christ and anyway, on his death these thoughts were dominating in him. The anecdote is famous of the nocturnal visit of Vasari, in Rome, to the great old man who was actually sculpting this Pietà: the door was opened at the conventional knock of the Aretino, Michelangelo appeared with a lamp in his hand, and Vasari explained the request for a drawing on the part of the Pope. Michelangelo then sent the faithful Urbino upstairs and meanwhile, a leg of the group under work caugh Vasari's eye, which he was preparing to copy, as he was looking around. Well, jealous as always of his secret, Michelangelo pretended to drop the lantern and in the dark produced, he called Urbino, who brought a lamp; meanwhile he drew Vasari away from the vicinity of the statue and commented: « I am so old that often death pulls me by the coat because I am getting dry: and one day my person will fall, like this lantern, and the light of my life will be extinguished ».

In the Pietà of Palestrina (fig. 63; Academy of Florence) — not recorded in antique documents, and not accepted by various scholars as the work of Buonarroti — the ponderous collapsing mass of the dead Christ seems to be supported with difficulty by the two grieving persons, and the figures are delineated among elementary parallel contours, as in the Pauline Chapel. Finally, the Rondanini Pietà (fig. 70; Museum of the Castello Sforzesco), was described in this way in the inventory of Michelangelo's Roman house: « another statue started for a Christ, with another above, attached together, sketched and unfinished ». The artist had worked on it until the eve of his death, changing the placing in certain points, (for the first arrangement, there is the testimony of a drawing at Oxford), like the fine result of the right arm left unattached to the body. In the Rondanini Pietà, something medieval, and at the same time, very modern, chains the work to its time, in the Renaissance conception, in a surpassing of the form towards expression which is only of the spirit, and in the two exhausted figures, embracing from a profoundity of struggling sentiment, they almost fuse together.

THE ROMAN ARCHITECTURE AND THE END: *The Architectural Works*
The Last Works.

Towards the middle of the century, Michelangelo had also carried out great architectural works. From 1546, there was the completion of the Farnese Palace (the impressive large entablature on the exterior; and the third floor of the courtyard, which is much more dynamic than the two preceding ones by Sangallo); the same year saw the start of the systematisation of Piazza del Campidoglio (the use of the gigantesque Corinthian types in the Palazzo Senatorio and of the other two lateral ones which flank it; and the powerful unity around to the central space with the equestrian statue); and from 1547 he was the chief architect of St. Peters. In this way, the church in which he was unable to place the sepulcre of Julius II, and in which he had seen Bramante triumph, finished in his hands; but he now recognised the genius of the Bramantesque project (« clear, subtle and luminous ») and had rather to combat with its dishonest continuers (the « Sangallo set »). Consequently, Buonarroti wanted a return to the Greek cross, cutting all the external perimeter of the temple with a great order placed above with an attic; in the facade there would have been a pronaos and a portico; and on the four lateral minor domes, would have dominated the main Dome, with a double semi-dome like the one in Florence, but differently plastic and decorated, and also it would have been hemispheric (in the original project, then modified by Della Porta), and sealed by all the Basilica.

In the meantime new popes were coming to succession, while Michelangelo continued his very temperate life in the little house of Macel dei Corvi, waiting for the death which was painted at the top of stairs in his house, but which seemed to wish to make him wait. In time he was tormented by gallstones of the bladder. In the epoch of Julius III (1550-55), Buonarroti carried out the projects for S. Giovanni dei Fiorentini, and he offered himself to Ignatius di Loyola, asking him to give him the project of the church of Gesù, « just for devotion ». Under Paul IV (1555-59) the narrow counter-reformatism was made tighter and the Inquisition menaced; in the Last Judgement of the Sistine Chapel, the scabrous nudity was covered, while Michelangelo was even accused of being a Lutheran. One reaction came under the pontifship following of Pius IV (1559-65), a great patron who entrusted other architectural commissions to Buonarroti: the reconstruction of the gates into Rome, of which only the Porta Pia was carried out, (1561; compare fig. 69); the transformation of the Diocletian Baths into the church and convent of Santa Maria degli Angeli (1536-66); and the Sforza Chapel (1564). Michelangelo rose at sunrise to go to his work, but he also sculpted into the heart of night, by the light of a candle fixed to a cardboard hat placed on his head, attacking the marble with incredible force. At the age of eighty one he wrote to Vasari that it was midnight, and that death was sculpted in every one of his thoughts, but that he could not return to Florence so as not to abandon the construction of

St. Peters, which many longed to take over from him. He cited —
although « many say that I have grown childish » — the very beautiful
sonnet which begins:

> « *The span of life has run its course...* »

finishing:

> « *Neither to paint nor sculpt does not quieten anymore*
> *The soul turned to that divine love*
> *Which opens its arms to take us in its embrace* ».

On the 14th January 1564, at almost ninety, he finally became ill,
dying at sunset on the 18th, present were Tommaso Cavalieri, Daniele
da Volterra and two docters. The body, deposited in S.S. Apostoli in
Rome, was straight afterwards secretely taken away, however, by his
nephew to Florence, where it arrived on March 10th charging great
emotion. On July 14th the Academy of Drawing celebrated his very
solemn funeral in San Lorenzo, the church of the Medici: in 1570
the monumental tomb in S. Croce would have been finished on a design
by Vasari and the work was carried out by others.

[Handwritten marginal notes:]

NB.

Picasso: "At twelve I could draw like Raphael, it took me a lifetime to paint like a child"

"The comedy is over..." Beethoven.

Beethoven: "I will not leave this Earth until I have created everything I feel destined to create." Then what? "The comedy is over"

1. "Flat-technique" — from Donatello. Veiled figure — inspired by classical tomb. Face absorbed — foreboding thought [Holding the funeral sheet of Christ — servants on stairs] (Putti) — inevitability? Fate → "divine love" — men must be "perfect" — humanism? illusion Michelangelo true bodies — athletic, Michelangelo only a young boy. Composition tight.
2. Subject suggested by Poliziano. Unity of enveloping, swirling bodies

1. - *Madonna of the Stair* (Florence - Buonarroti House)

2. - Battle of the Centaurs (Florence - Buonarroti House)

3. - Angel Candelabra
(Bologna - San Domenico)

4. - *Crucifixion* (Florence - Buonarroti House)

5. - *Bacchus* (Florence - Bargello National Museum)

6. - *Madonna of Bruges* (Bruges - Nôtre-Dame)

7. - *Pietà* (Rome - St. Peter)

8. - *Pietà* - Detail of the face of Christ

9. - *Pietà* - Detail of the face of the Madonna

10.-11. - *David*
(Florence -
Academy Gallery)

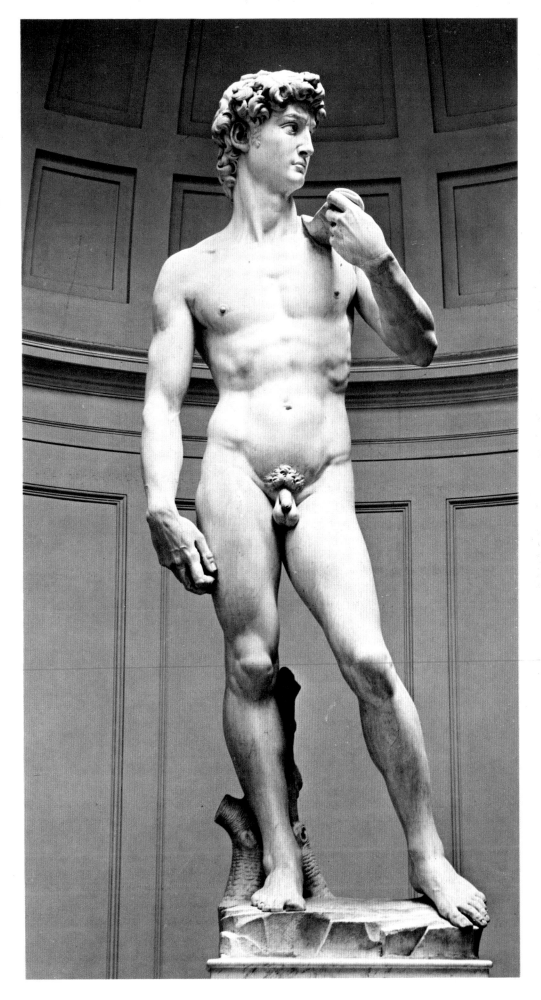

12. - *Madonna with Infant (Pitti Tondo)* (Florence - Bargello National Museum)

13. - *Sacred Family (Doni Tondo)* (Florence - Uffizi Gallery)

14. - *Madonna with Infant (Taddei Tondo)* (London - Royal Academy)

15. - *St. Matthew* (Florence - Academy Gallery)

16. - General view of the *Sistine Chapel* (Vatican Museums)

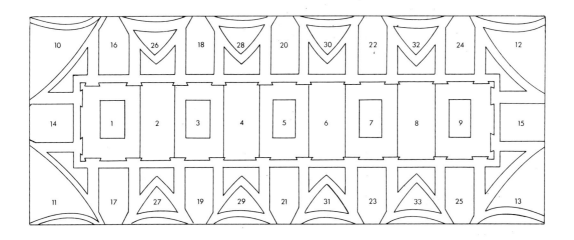

LOS FRESCOS DE MIGUEL-ANGEL DE LA BOVEDA DE LA CAPILLA SIXTINA

1 - La separación de la luz de las tinieblas.

2 - La creación del sol y de la luna.

3 - La separación de las aguas.

4 - La creación del hombre.

5 - La creación de la mujer.

6 - El pecado original y el destierro del paraíso terrestre.

7 - El sacrificio de Noé.

8 - El diluvio universal.

9 - La embriaguez de Noé.

10 - Aman crucifijo por orden de Ester.

11 - Los hebreos acometidos por los serpientes enviados por Dios.

12 - David en el acto de decapitar Goliat.

13 - Judith con la cabeza de Holofernes.

14 - El Profeta Jonás.

15 - El Profeta Zacarías.

16 - El Profeta Jeremías.

17 - La Sibila Líbica.

18 - La Sibila Pérsica.

19 - El Profeta Daniel.

20 - El Profeta Ecequiel.

21 - La Sibila Cumana.

22 - La Sibila Eritrea.

23 - El Profeta Isaías.

24 - El Profeta Joel.

25 - La Sibila Délfica.

26 - Salomón niño con su madre.

27 - El futuro rey Jese con sus padres.

28 - Roboam niño con su madre.

29 - Asa niño con sus padres.

30 - Ocia niño con sus padres y un hermano.

31 - Ecequías niño con sus padres.

32 - Zorobabel niño con sus padres.

33 - Josía niño con sus padres.

17. - Sistine Chapel - *The Original Sin and the Expulsion from Paradise*

19. - Sistine Chapel - *God dividing Light from Darkness* (detail)

18. - Sistine Chapel - *The Creation of Man*

DANIEL

20. - Sistine Chapel - *The Prophet Daniel*

21. - Sistine Chapel - *The Libyan Sibyl*

LIBICA

22. - Sistine Chapel - *The Delphic Sibyl*

IOEL

23. - Sistine Chapel - *The Prophet Joel*

24. - Sistine Chapel - *The Erythraean Sibyl*

25. - Sistine Chapel - *The Prophet Zachariah*

CVMAEA

26. - Sistine Chapel - *The Cumaean Sibyl*

27. - Sistine Chapel - *The Prophet Ezekiel*

28. - *Dying Prisoner* (Paris - Louvre)

29. - *Rebelling Prisoner* (Paris - Louvre)

30. - *Tomb of Julius II* (Rome - San Pietro in Vincoli). In the centre
the *Moses,* at the sides the statues of *Rachel* (right) and *Lea* (left)

31.-32. - *The Moses*

33. - *Awakening Prisoner*

34. - *The youthful Prisoner*

35. - *Prisoner called « Atlantis »*

36. - *The bearded Prisoner*

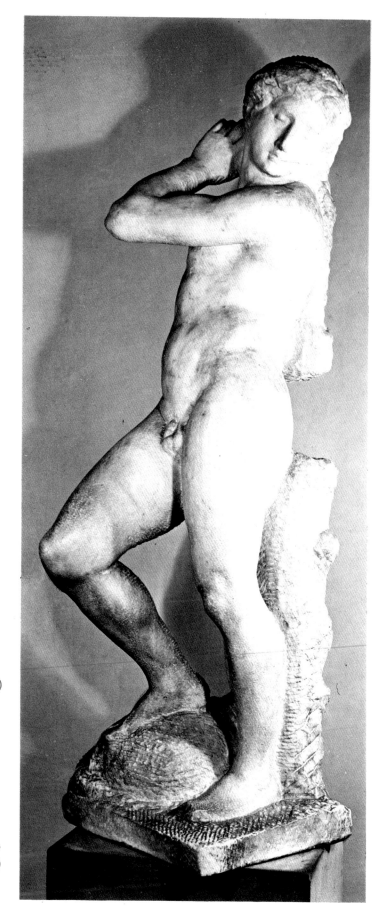

37. - *Christ Risen* (or *Bearing the Cross*)
(Rome - Santa Maria sopra Minerva)

38. - *The David Apollo*
(Florence - Bargello National Museaum)

39. - General view of the *New Sacristy* in San Lorenzo (Florence)

40. - *Madonna with Infant*
(The New Sacristy)

41.-42. - *Statue and Tomb of Lorenzo, Duke of Urbino* (The New Sacristy)

43. - Tomb of Lorenzo - *Statue of Evening*

44. - Tomb of Lorenzo - *Statue of Dawn*

47. - Tomb of Giuliano - *Statue of Night*

48. - Tomb of Giuliano - *Statue of Day*

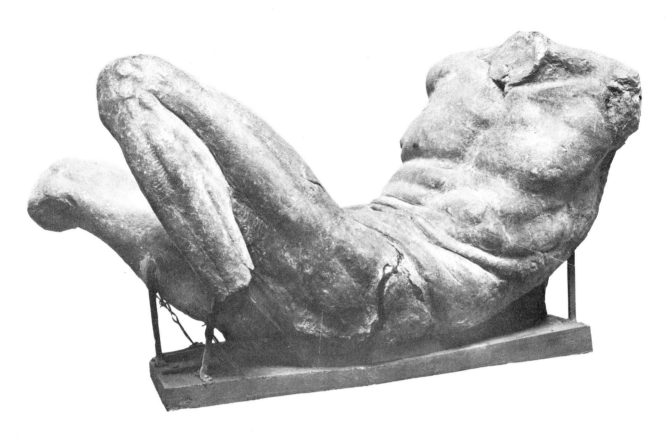

49. - *Model of River* (Florence - Buonarroti House)

50. - *Inclining Youth*
(Leningrado - The Eremitage)

51. - *The Victory*
(Florence - The Palazzo Vecchio)

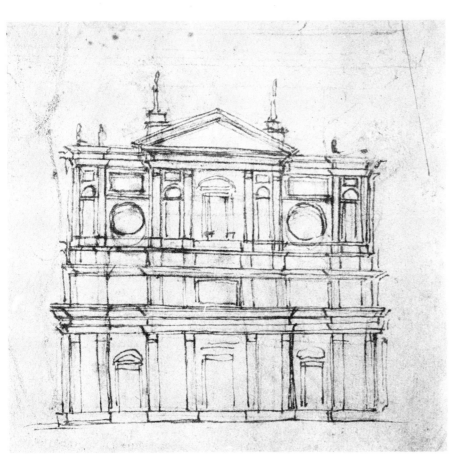

52. - *Model for the façade
of the Church of San Lorenzo*
(Florence - Buonarroti House)

54. - *Drawing for the fortificatior
of Floren.*
(Florence - Buonarroti Hous

53. - *Hall and stairs of the
Laurenziana Library* (Florence)

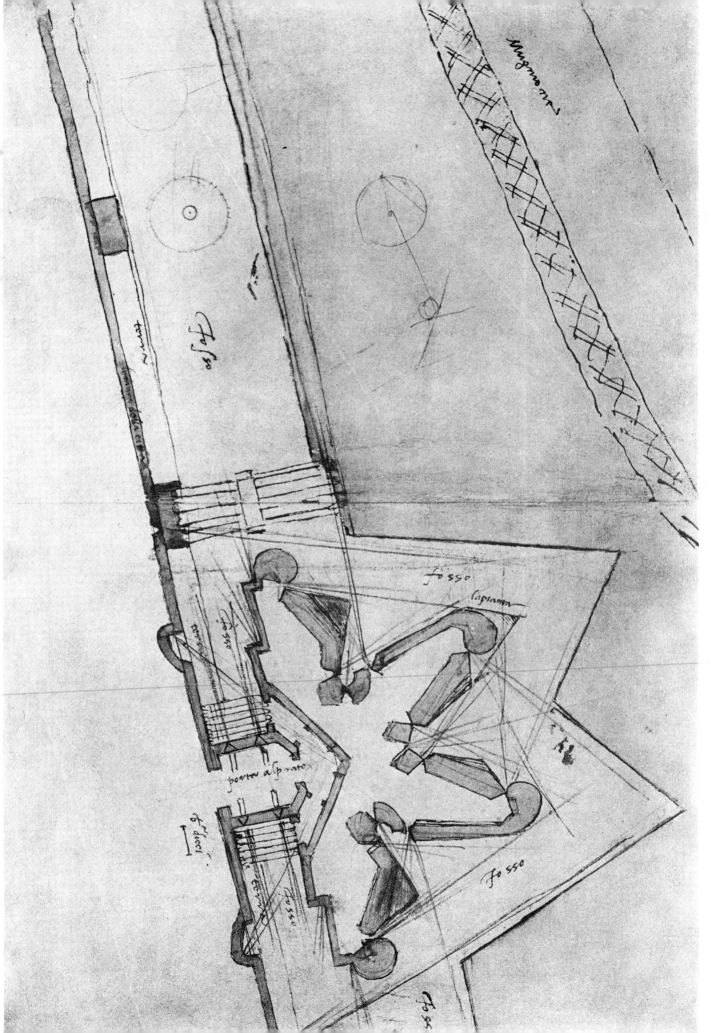

55. - *Bust of Brutus* (Florence - Bargello National Museum)

56. - *The Last Judgment* (Sistine Chapel - Vatican Museums)

57. - Detail of the *Last Judgment*

58. - *Christ the Judge* - Detail of the Last Judgment

59. - *The Fall of St. Paul* (The Paolina Chapel - Vatican Museums)

60. - *Crucifixion of St. Peter* (The Paolina Chapel - Vatican Muséums)

61.-62. - *Pietà* (Florence - Cathedral of Santa Maria del Fiore)

63. - *The Pietà of Palestrina* (Florence - Academy Gallery)

64.-65. - *Michelangelo's plan for the systematization of the Campidoglio reppresented in two etchings of 1567 and 1568*

66. - *Drawing for the plan of the Church of San Giovanni dei Florentines in Rome (Florence - Buonarroti House)*

67. - *Courtyard of the Farnese Palace in an etching of 1560*

68. - *Dome of St. Peter's Basilica*

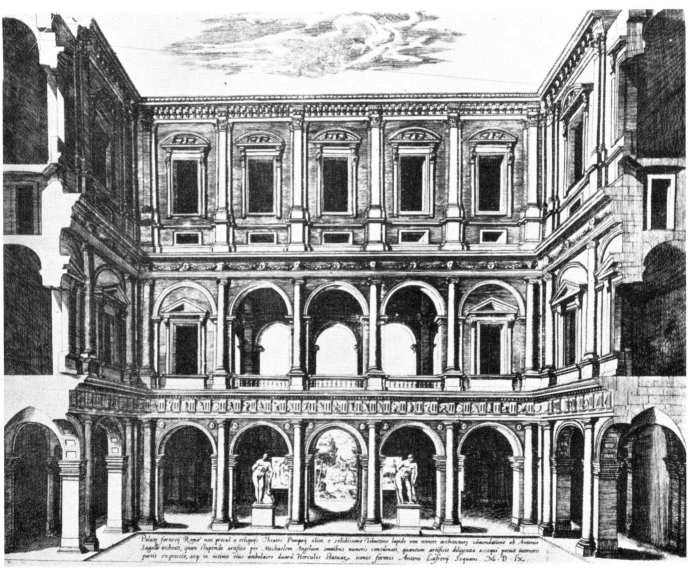

69. - *Drawing for the Porta Pia in Rome* (Florence - Buonarroti House)

70. - *Rondanini Pietà* (Milan - Sforzesco Castle).

Stampato in Firenze

Arti Grafiche PARIGI & MAGGIORELLI